A Guide for Using

Johnny Appleseed

in the Classroom

Based on the novel written by Stephen Kellogg

*This guide written by **Nancy Phillips***

Teacher Created Resources, Inc.
6421 Industry Way
Westminster, CA 92683
www.teachercreated.com

©1995 Teacher Created Resources, Inc.
Reprinted, 2005

Made in U.S.A.
ISBN-1-55734-536-8

Edited by
Dona Herwick Rice

Illustrated by
Kathy Bruce

Cover Art by
Charles Ketcham

Table of Contents

Introduction and Sample Lesson Plan 3

Getting to Know the Book and Author 4

Suggestions for Using the Unit Activities 5

Unit Activities—Language Arts

❖ Bulletin Board Activity 10

❖ Apple and Leaf Patterns 11

❖ Story Questions 12

❖ Make a Flip Booklet 13

❖ Story Summary Sentence Strips 14

❖ Who's Johnny? 15

❖ My Special Place 16

❖ Friendship Tree 17

❖ True or Tall? 18

❖ A Tall Tale 20

❖ A Journal for Johnny 21

❖ Safety First! 22

❖ Pack Your Back 23

❖ Stranger, Danger, Friend, or Foe? 25

❖ Dear Ma and Pa 26

❖ Alike and Different 27

❖ Just for Fun 28

❖ Vocabulary Quiz 29

Unit Activities—Related Curriculum

❖ What's Inside? 30

❖ An Apple a Day 31

❖ Good "NUT"rition 32

❖ Food Guide Pyramid 33

❖ Recipe for Applesauce 34

❖ Apple Dolls 35

❖ Johnny's Forest Friends 36

❖ Where Is That? 37

❖ Movin' On! 39

❖ What Would Johnny Do? 40

❖ Nutty Gameboard 42

❖ *Johnny Appleseed* Readers' Theater 43

❖ Music and Poetry 46

Bibliography 47

Answer Key 48

Introduction and Sample Lesson Plan

A good book can touch the lives of children like a good friend. The pictures, words, themes, and characters can inspire young minds as they turn to literary treasures for companionship, recreation, comfort, and guidance.

Johnny Appleseed is a timeless favorite for young children. As a folktale, it incorporates the basic themes of friendship, courage, and responsibility. In addition, the story can be easily woven into existing units on folk heroes, apples, trees, nutrition, safety and survival, peacemaking, development of a town, Colonial America, forests, and forest animals. The following literature unit is intended for use in the primary grades and offers a variety of activities from which to choose, depending on grade level, existing curriculum, and related themes. Opportunities exist for individual creativity, cooperative learning, and class projects.

Among the objectives of the unit are to introduce the students to positive character traits, to reinforce critical thinking skills through a variety of literature-based activities, to gain practice in oral and written language, to expand knowledge of peacemaking strategies, and to learn methods of safety and survival. The literature unit also includes the integration of the curriculum with activities in social studies, health, science, math, cooking, art, music, and drama.

Teachers who use this literature unit to supplement their own valuable ideas can plan the activities using the following sample lesson plan or a lesson plan of their own.

Lesson 1
- Introduce the book by using some or all of unit activities #2 and #3 on page 5.
- Read "About the Author" (page 4) with the students.
- Discuss the vocabulary words (page 5).
- Have the students hang apple vocabulary words on the tree, using activity #4 on page 5.
- Discuss the concepts of friendship, courage, and responsibility (#5, #6, and #7, page 6).
- Prepare for reading the story by completing unit activities #8 and #9 on page 6.

Lesson 2
- Read the story a second time.
- Prepare a bulletin board, using the story questions (pages 10-12).
- Make a flip booklet, using the sentence strips (pages 13 and 14).
- Present vocabulary words for the word puzzle (page 28) and duplicate a copy of the page for each student to complete.
- Design a travel poster (page 39).
- Write a journal entry for Johnny (page 21).

Lesson 3
- Complete "Who's Johnny?" (page 15).
- Complete "Alike and Different" (page 27).
- Begin "A Friendship Tree" (page 17).
- Practice map skills (pages 37 and 38).
- Complete "True or Tall?" (pages 18 and 19).
- Have the students write tall tales (page 20).
- Begin practicing the readers' theater (pages 43-45).
- Begin making apple dolls (page 35).

Lesson 4
- Introduce survival themes with "Pack Your Back" (pages 23 and 24).
- Have the students design a new outfit for Johnny (#19, page 7).
- Complete "Safety First!" (page 22).
- Complete "Stranger, Danger, Friend, or Foe?" (page 25).
- Write a postcard home (page 26).
- Use math facts to play the "Nutty Gameboard" (page 42).
- Practice the poem and song (page 46).

Lesson 5
- Discuss apples and nuts. Review the "Food Guide Pyramid" (page 33).
- Complete the "What's Inside?" apple experiment (page 30).
- Assign apple and nut groups for research and work sheets (pages 31 and 32).
- Make applesauce (page 34).
- Complete the graphing activity (page 36).
- Continue practicing the readers' theater (pages 43-45).

Lesson 6
- Complete "Friendship Tree" (page 17).
- Have the students draw their special place (page 16).
- Complete the conflict resolution activity (pages 40 and 41).
- Complete the apple dolls (page 35).
- Give the vocabulary quiz (page 29).
- Present the readers' theater (pages 43-45) as a culminating activity.

Getting to Know the Book and Author

About the Author

Steven Kellogg was born on October 26, 1941, in Norwalk, Connecticut. From the time he was a child, he always enjoyed drawing animals and birds.

As a young man, Mr. Kellogg earned a degree from the Rhode Island School of Design. During his senior year of college, he studied in Italy on a special fellowship. This experience led him to decide to become a professional artist.

Mr. Kellogg began illustrating books in 1967 and has won many awards for his action-filled illustrations. Some of his best known books are *Pecos Bill, Paul Bunyan,* and *Chicken Little.*

Steven Kellogg now lives in Sandy Hook, Connecticut.

About the Book

(Johnny Appleseed is published in the U.S. by William Morrow, in Canada by Gage Distributors, in the U.K by International Book Distributors, and in Australia by Kirby Book Co.)

Johnny Appleseed is a popular folktale about the life of John Chapman, a man who lived from 1774-1845. Born in Leominster, Massachusetts, John loved apple trees and apples.

As John watched apples grow, he became very interested in all of nature. He often played in the nearby forest and made friends with animals. The forest was a very peaceful place for Johnny.

As soon as he was old enough, John traveled west to Ohio, planting apple orchards for new settlers. Along the way, as an explorer and adventurer, he cleared forests, slept and played with animals, befriended Indians and other strangers, and survived many dangers. Johnny was so well-loved and respected by all who knew him that over the years legends spread about the man whom everyone came to call Johnny Appleseed.

Suggestions for Using the Unit Activities

Johnny Appleseed is a book that can be used to introduce a number of themes. The following are some suggestions for setting the stage.

- Display *Johnny Appleseed* along with other folktales such as *Paul Bunyan* and *Pecos Bill*. Discuss what makes a folktale.
- Display different versions of *Johnny Appleseed* by different authors. Compare and contrast.
- Display various books by the same author and let the students explain their similarities and differences.

1. Before you begin the unit, prepare vocabulary cards (words and pattern below or page 11), sentence strips (page 14), the bulletin board (pages 10-11 and #10 on page 6), and the questions (page 12). Make the vocabulary tree. (See #4 below.)

2. Initiate a discussion of apples and apple orchards by asking the students if they have ever been apple picking. Ask what their favorite foods are that have apples in them. Show pictures of apple pie, applesauce, and apple cake.

3. Ask if anyone can locate Massachusetts. Find it on a map. Show where Leominster is in relation to Boston. Now show Pennsylvania, Ohio, the Allegheny Mountains, and Indiana.

4. Make a vocabulary apple tree. Obtain a large dead limb with many branches on it. Secure it in a bucket of sand. Print each vocabulary word on a red apple shape (pattern below and on page 11) and punch a hole at the top. String the apples with green yarn. As each word is introduced and the meaning is discussed in context, the students can take turns hanging the apples on the tree.

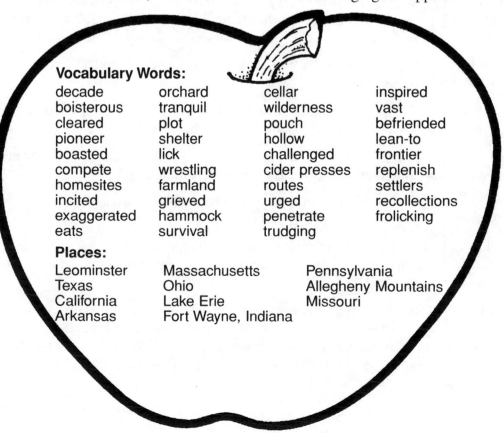

Vocabulary Words:

decade	orchard	cellar	inspired
boisterous	tranquil	wilderness	vast
cleared	plot	pouch	befriended
pioneer	shelter	hollow	lean-to
boasted	lick	challenged	frontier
compete	wrestling	cider presses	replenish
homesites	farmland	routes	settlers
incited	grieved	urged	recollections
exaggerated	hammock	penetrate	frolicking
eats	survival	trudging	

Places:

Leominster	Massachusetts	Pennsylvania
Texas	Ohio	Allegheny Mountains
California	Lake Erie	Missouri
Arkansas	Fort Wayne, Indiana	

Suggestions for Using the Unit Activities *(cont.)*

5. Have the students give their ideas on friendship. What makes a good friend? Tell about someone you think is a good friend and why.

6. Ask what courage is and if anyone can give an example of a time that he/she showed courage.

7. What does it mean to be responsible? What are some examples of showing responsibility? Discuss responsibility for oneself and for others.

8. Display the cover of *Johnny Appleseed*. Have the students tell if the story takes place now or long ago. How can they tell? Where is Johnny? Why would he be called *Johnny Appleseed*? Do you think that is his real name?

9. Read the story aloud.

10. Develop critical thinking skills with the story questions (page 12). They are based on Bloom's Taxonomy. Use the leaf pattern (page 11) and write one question on each leaf. As each question is answered, write the answer on an apple using the apple pattern (page 11). Each student places an apple on the appropriate question on the tree bulletin board.

11. Make a flip booklet (page 13). Have the students cut apart the sentence strips (page 14) and place them in the correct order on the bottom of each page. Illustrate each sentence.

12. Use the character map (page 15) to have the students decide on words that describe Johnny. Each student is to write a sentence for each word that describes Johnny.

13. Discuss where Johnny went when he wanted to find peace. Each student can answer questions and draw his/her own special place (page 16).

14. Discuss qualities that make a good friend and encourage the students to tell about their special friends. In the tree, each student is to write about his/her best friend (page 17).

15. Discuss the differences between fact and fantasy and what a tall tale is. The students are to cut out the statements and glue them under the right heading on the following page (pages 18 and 19).

16. Discuss characteristics of tall tales and have each student make up a tall tale to read to the class (page 20).

17. Duplicate a copy of page 21 for everyone. Have each student write a journal entry for one day in Johnny's travels. Each student must write from Johnny's point of view and describe his/her favorite adventure from the story.

18. Page 22 provides an opportunity to discuss how Johnny knew so much about surviving alone. Discuss the ways he survived (such as eating butternuts, taking shelter, not getting lost) and how he knew what to do. Divide the class into groups and provide opportunities for the children to brainstorm safety and survival techniques. Each group can provide a list. Together, the class can prepare one safety chart to share with another class.

Suggestions for Using the Unit Activities *(cont.)*

19. Continue a discussion of survival and encourage the students to think and prioritize what they would take with them if they were going on a hiking trip (page 23). The students can work either individually or in small groups to decide what they would bring. Younger children can just choose items from the list on page 24 and be prepared to explain their choices. Older children can use weights to figure even more logically. An additional activity can be to design a new outfit for Johnny.

20. Discuss being friendly to strangers. Have the students answer questions concerning safety and protection. Complete the activity on page 25 and have the students compile a list of rules for self-protection. Present the children with various situations and ask for responses. For example, ask what they would do in the following situation: You are home alone, and someone rings the doorbell. You cannot see who it is from the window. You ask who it is. The person says that he is a police officer. What should you do?

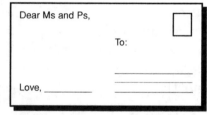

21. Have the children write postcards as if they were Johnny writing home to his family (page 26). What would he like to tell them? Duplicate the postcard form on heavy construction paper and have each student draw a picture on the other side.

22. Complete a Venn diagram (page 27) comparing Johnny and another folk hero, Paul Bunyan.

23. Duplicate a copy of page 28 for each child. Before starting, go over the vocabulary words on the page.

24. Use page 29 for a fill-in-the-blanks vocabulary quiz.

25. Page 30 is a science lesson using the scientific method, whereby the students make observations and draw conclusions.

Suggestions for Using the Unit Activities *(cont.)*

26. Activities on apple and nut nutrition can be presented (pages 31 and 32). The following information is for teacher use.

> **Apple** (medium)   **Nuts** (1 oz./25 g)
> 80 calories   170 calories
> 3 g fiber   16 g fiber
> 160 mg. potassium   180 mg. potassium
> vitamin C   protein
> beta-carotene   19 g fat

Apples are high in vitamin C and have almost no saturated fat, cholesterol, or sodium. They have high soluble fiber content, about 25% of which is in the form of pectin which lowers blood cholesterol levels by reducing the absorption of fats. An apple is a natural toothbrush since it is fibrous, juicy, and not sticky. It also helps to clear away food debris through the mechanical act of eating.

Nuts contain chemicals that prevent cancer in animals. They regulate the blood sugar and are high in trace minerals (zinc, copper, iron, calcium, magnesium, and phosphorous). They are also high in fats and calories. Nuts are thought to have some value in fighting heart disease. They cause allergic reactions in some people. Butternuts are in the walnut family and have a very wrinkled shell. They are elliptical in shape and are about two inches (5 cm) long and one inch (2.5 cm) across. They grow in groups of two to five.

Divide the class into two groups: Apples and Nuts. Have each group research nutritional facts and set up a learning center with its food. The students can bring in pictures, actual samples, and make charts. Due to allergic reactions, do not allow the children to bring in samples of nuts for tasting. Make a comparison chart of apples and nuts.

Additional information about food can be found on page 33.

27. Prepare a cooking lesson using the recipe for applesauce on page 34. This is also an opportunity to reinforce the concepts of following directions and sequencing in addition to learning cooking vocabulary. Cut apart the recipe strips and have the students place them in the correct order.

28. The students can use the directions on page 35 to make apple dolls. These will take approximately two weeks to complete due to the drying process.

29. Duplicate the picture of the forest animals (page 36). Mark the graph showing how many of each animal are found. Answer the questions at the bottom of the page.

30. The students can complete pages 37 and 38 to locate places of importance in the book and to review basic map skills involving location and direction.

31. Design a travel poster (page 39). Discuss the reasons for people moving westward during the 1800s. What were they leaving? What did they expect to find in their new locations?

Suggestions for Using the Unit Activities *(cont.)*

32. The activity on pages 40 and 41 focuses on peacemaking skills. Review how Johnny behaved with the Indians with whom he did not share the same language. Also review how he managed the group of woodsmen who challenged him to a wrestling match. Cut apart the conflict strips and distribute different problems to each group. Create a set of resolution cards for each group with words such as share, take turns, compromise, use humor, apologize, change, and ignore it. The students can decide how to handle a conflict and then hold up the appropriate resolution card.

33. Make a copy of the gameboard on page 42 for each student. Either cut out nut shapes from construction paper or use real walnut halves for each student. The gameboard can be used for math facts or vocabulary. The teacher or caller will say a math fact. The first person to raise his hand and say the correct answer places a nut on his gameboard. The first person to cover the gameboard with nuts is the winner. Variation: Play in groups and assign a caller.

34. The students can create their own play from the script on pages 43-45. It can be presented for another class, and apple invitations can be made. (Use the apple pattern on page 11.) The students can also design and make theater admission tickets.

35. "Old Brass Wagon" is a song that was sung during Johnny's days. It is said that children in Indiana still sing it after they are finished picking apples. The lyrics and an additional poem about apples are included on page 46.

36. Additional activities might include the following:

   • solving math word problems involving apples
   • designing a book jacket
   • making dried apple snacks
   • creating a class newspaper
   • writing and/or acting out interviews with Johnny Appleseed
   • creating a class mural

Bulletin Board Activity

The following directions are for making a "Tree of Knowledge" bulletin board.

Materials:

- patterns (page 11)
- pen or colored markers
- stapler, tacks, and/or glue

- scissors
- pencil
- light blue, brown, green, and red construction paper

Directions for Making the Bulletin Board:

Prepare the bulletin board by covering it with light blue paper. Using brown construction paper, cut out the shape of a tree. Make only the trunk and branches and attach them to the blue background. Then, using the leaf and apple patterns, make leaves and apples from green and red construction paper. Cut out an equal number of each to correspond to the number of questions on page 12. Write the questions on the leaves with pen or colored marker. Write each answer on an apple, also using either pen or colored marker.

Directions for Using the Bulletin Board:

Read a leaf question and call on someone to answer.

Example:

> Question: *What did Johnny do when he ran out of apple seeds?*
> Answer: *He hiked back to the eastern cider presses.*

The student who answers correctly places the question leaf on the tree and the apple answer at the base of the leaf. You can also have the first student who answers correctly call on the next person. The students can also work in pairs.

When you are finished, you will have a colorful bulletin board of an apple tree covered with leaves and apples. The students can refer to the board if they have any questions.

Note: Make additional leaves and apples and create additional questions as you see fit.

Apple and Leaf Patterns

Cut out the patterns and use them for the vocabulary and question trees. (See pages 5, 6, and 10.)

Story Questions

The following questions are based on Bloom's Taxonomy. To use the questions, first prepare the leaves (page 11) as directed. Write a different question on each leaf. Use the same pattern page to prepare apple shapes, and on each apple write the answer to one question.

I. Knowledge

- What inspired in Johnny a love of all nature?
- Where did Johnny find shelter when a storm struck?
- On what did Johnny survive in the winter?
- What did Johnny do when he ran out of apple seeds?
- Where did Johnny plant apple orchards?

II. Comprehension

- Do you think the story takes place now or long ago? Why?
- Why do you think the animals were so gentle with Johnny?
- In what ways do you think winters slowed Johnny down?
- How did Johnny know so much about surviving alone in the woods?

III. Application

- How did Johnny feel when he got the woodsmen to chop down the trees? How did he show he was smart?
- What would have happened if the settlers had not traveled along the route that Johnny predicted?
- What are some ways that you are a good friend?
- What would you like to plant to make people happy? Why?

IV. Analysis

- Why do you think it was so important to Johnny to move out west before the settlers arrived?
- How did people show that they really liked Johnny?
- How did Johnny live like a king in the woods? What was better for him there than in a house?

V. Synthesis

- Would the story have been different if it had taken place in a different part of the country? Tell how.
- How did Johnny show that he had courage? Does that mean that he was never afraid? Why or why not?

VI. Evaluation

- Do you think Johnny liked being called Johnny Appleseed? Why or why not?
- Why did people like to exaggerate stories about Johnny?
- Do you think Johnny was happy with the way he lived his life? Why or why not?
- Would you recommended this book to a friend? Why or why not?

Make a Flip Booklet

Materials:

- four sheets standard-size paper per student
- long-armed stapler
- scissors
- glue
- page 14 (one copy per student)
- crayons or markers

Directions: Give each student four sheets of paper. Fold each in the following ways:

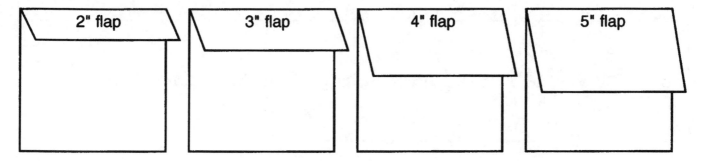

Place all folds together and staple them as shown.

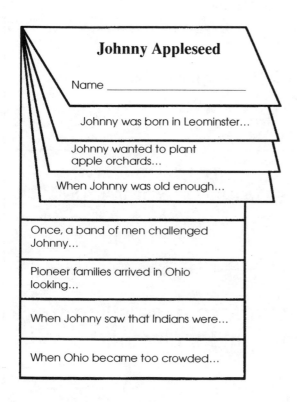

Have the students cut out the summary strips (page 14) and place them in their correct order. Glue each strip to the bottom of each flap and illustrate the scene that is described. Use the 2" (5 cm) flap for title and name.

Story Summary Sentence Strips

Pioneer families arrived in Ohio looking for homesites and farmland.

When Ohio became too crowded, Johnny moved to Indiana.

Johnny wanted to plant apple orchards for new settlers.

Johnny was born in Leominster, Massachusetts.

When Johnny saw that Indians were attacking the settlers, he shouted a warning at every door.

When Johnny was old enough, he set out to explore the great wilderness to the west.

Once, a band of men challenged Johnny to a wrestling match. He suggested a tree-chopping match instead.

Name _____   Date _____

Who's Johnny?

Think about what Johnny was like and the things that Johnny did. Below is a picture of Johnny. On the lines next to the picture, write words that describe him.

Extension: Use each word in a sentence that describes Johnny. Make sure that you give examples to support your opinion of Johnny.

Name _____   Date _____

My Special Place

Answer questions 1 and 2 below. Then, follow the directions for number 3.

1. Where did Johnny go when it was noisy at his house?

_____

2. Why did Johnny enjoy going there?

_____

_____

3. Draw a place where you like to go that makes you happy.

Name _____   Date _____

Friendship Tree

Johnny Appleseed was a good friend and everyone liked him.

Tell about someone you like. What makes this person a good friend? Write your answer in the tree.

True or Tall?

Cut out the sentences below. Glue each under the correct heading on the next page. (Tall means a stretch of the truth.)

You can pick apples from trees.
You can walk hundreds of miles barefoot in the snow without harm.
You can talk to birds, and they will understand.
You can survive on butternuts and apples.
You can keep a wild wolf for a pet.
You can sometimes outsmart troublemakers.
You can make friends with strangers.
People still see Johnny Appleseed today.
You can make applesauce, cider, and vinegar from apples.
The skin on your feet can be so tough a rattlesnake cannot bite through it.
You can store apples in a cool cellar to eat all winter.
You can play with bears that you meet in a forest.

Name _____   Date _____

True or Tall? *(cont.)*

True

Tall

Name _____   Date _____

A Tall Tale

The story of Johnny Appleseed is a tall tale. Make up a tall tale of your own to read to the class.

Name _____ Date _____

A Journal for Johnny

Johnny decided to keep a journal while he traveled to Ohio. This was so that he would remember all the interesting events that happened to him.

Write an entry for the day you think was Johnny's most exciting adventure. Remember to put yourself in Johnny's place and write from his point-of-view.

March 1, 1795

_____

_____

_____

_____

_____

_____

_____

_____

_____

_____

_____

Name _____   Date _____

Safety First!

Johnny Appleseed knew a lot about taking care of himself when he was alone. Answer the following questions to show what Johnny knew.

1. What did Johnny do in a snowstorm?

   _____

   _____

2. What did Johnny eat in the winter when he was hungry?

   _____

   _____

3. Why did Johnny not get lost?

   _____

   _____

Write some safety rules that **you** know.

Safety Rules

1. _____

   _____

2. _____

   _____

3. _____

   _____

4. _____

   _____

Name _____ Date _____

Pack Your Back

Look at the list on the next page. Choose which items on the list you think Johnny Appleseed would take with him on a long journey if he were alive today. Finally, answer the following question:

Johnny weighs 165 lbs. (75 kg). The most he should carry on a long hike is one-third of his body weight. How much would that be? (Note: Johnny's backpack weighs 3 lbs. or 1.5 kg)

Pack Your Back *(cont.)*

sleeping bag—1 lb. 10 oz. (750 g)

tent—3 lbs. (1.35 kg)

matches—1 oz. (25 g)

shovel—3 lbs. 1 oz. (1.5 kg)

candles—6 oz. (175 g)

knife—3 oz. (75 g)

sandals—2 lbs. (900 g)

first aid kit—12 oz. (350 g)

extra socks—12 oz. (350 g)

raincoat—12 oz. (350 g)

hat—4 oz. (100 g)

pans—2 lbs. (900 g)

binoculars—13 oz. (375 g)

string—2 oz. (50 g)

flashlight—9 oz. (275 g)

plates—5 oz. (125 g)

sewing kit—2 oz. (50 g)

food—1 lb. (450 g)

notebook—2 oz. (50 g)

gloves—3 oz. (75 9)

travel mug—8 oz. (225 g)

rubber raft—3 lbs. 8 oz. (1.5 kg)

axe—1 lb. 12 oz. (800 g)

rope—6 lbs. 4 oz. (2.8 kg)

apple seeds—10 lbs. (4.5 kg)

cooler—7 oz. (200 g)

sunscreen—3 oz. (75 g)

insect spray—2 oz. (50 g)

bug jacket—10 oz. (300 g)

small stove—9 lbs. (4 kg)

corn popper—1 lb. 3 oz. (525 g)

compass—3 oz. (75 g)

lantern—10 oz. (300 g)

sunglasses—2 oz. (50 g)

air mattress—1 lb. 12 oz. (800 g)

magnifying glass—1 oz. (25 g)

plastic bags—1 oz. (25 g)

canteen—5 oz. (125 g)

Teacher Note: The standard and metric measurements are not meant to be equivalent.

Name _____ Date _____

Stranger, Danger, Friend, or Foe?

Johnny loved to help people, and he always befriended strangers. It is good to be friendly, but you also have to be aware. It is important to be careful when you meet a stranger. Look at the pictures below and think about what you would do.

Now, work with a partner to come up with some safety rules for each of these situations. Afterwards, the whole class can share ideas.

• List some telephone safety rules that you know.

_____

_____

_____

• List some safety rules for when you are home alone.

_____

_____

_____

• List some safety rules for when you are outdoors by yourself.

_____

_____

_____

Name _____ Date _____

Dear Ma and Pa

Pretend that you are Johnny and writing a postcard home. Write it from Johnny's point-of-view and tell what you think his parents would want to know. Draw a picture on the other side for the front of the postcard.

_____
Date

Dear Ma and Pa,

_____

_____

_____

_____

_____

_____

_____

Love, _____

To:

_____

_____

_____

Name _____

Date _____

Alike and Different

Compare Johnny Appleseed with Paul Bunyan. How are they similar? How are they different? Complete the Venn diagram.

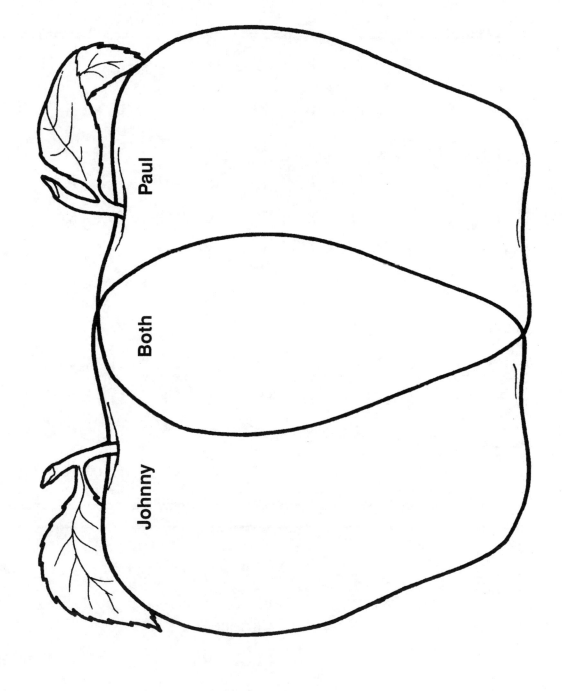

Johnny

Both

Paul

Name _____   Date _____

Just for Fun

Find the words listed at the bottom of the page in the puzzle. The words go across, (left to right), or down.

C	L	E	A	R	E	D	B	F	U	X	F	V	T
B	X	Y	N	B	M	R	Y	U	N	R	R	H	U
E	R	E	C	O	L	L	E	C	T	I	O	N	S
L	A	J	I	I	E	E	M	R	A	J	N	Y	H
O	C	B	D	S	J	A	G	B	M	N	T	Y	E
V	T	K	E	T	U	N	M	T	E	B	I	E	L
E	I	B	R	E	Y	T	C	D	D	M	E	X	T
D	C	F	P	R	N	O	X	Z	R	I	R	L	E
B	A	N	R	O	V	R	O	U	T	E	S	Z	R
R	L	J	E	U	T	R	U	D	G	I	N	G	K
V	F	M	S	S	K	G	R	I	E	V	E	D	S
J	K	E	S	W	I	L	D	E	R	N	E	S	S

beloved	grieved	shelter
wilderness	frontier	cleared
untamed	boisterous	cider press
trudging	route	recollections

Name _____ Date _____

Vocabulary Quiz

Choose the correct word for each sentence from the word box below.

1. Watching apples grow _____ in John a love of all nature.

2. Johnny's feet were so tough that a rattlesnake's fang could not_____ .

3. In the winter, Johnny survived on a diet of _____ .

4. The woodsmen _____ that they could lick their weight in wildcats.

5. The settlers retold Johnny's stories and even _____ them a bit.

6. When Johnny ran out of apple seeds, he hiked back to the eastern cider presses to _____ his supply.

7. It_____ Johnny that his friends were fighting.

8. After the war, people_____ Johnny to build a house and settle down.

9. Johnny often escaped from his boisterous household to go to the _____ woods.

10. Johnny loved to be outdoors in the _____ .

<table>
<tr><td colspan="3" align="center">Word Box</td></tr>
<tr><td>exaggerated</td><td>penetrate</td><td>grieved</td></tr>
<tr><td>inspired</td><td>butternuts</td><td>replenish</td></tr>
<tr><td>wilderness</td><td>tranquil</td><td>boasted</td></tr>
<tr><td></td><td>urged</td><td></td></tr>
</table>

Name _____   Date _____

What's Inside?

1. Draw what you think the inside of an apple looks like.

2. Get into groups. Each group will receive an apple. The teacher will slice each apple in half. What does it look like inside? Describe it with words and then draw a picture.

   _____

   _____

   _____

   _____

3. Record how many seeds are in each group's apple.

   Group A   Group B   Group C   Group D   Group E

   _____   _____   _____   _____   _____

4. As a group, what are your conclusions about the inside of an apple?

   _____

   _____

   _____

   _____

Name _____ Date _____

An Apple a Day

Research some facts about apples.

1. List some ways that apples are good for you.

   _____

   _____

   _____

   _____

   _____

2. How many calories are in one medium apple?

   _____

3. How much fat is in an apple?

   _____

4. Why is an apple called "nature's toothbrush?"

   _____

   _____

   _____

   _____

5. How many servings of fruit should you have each day? Use the Food Guide Pyramid (page 33).

   _____

Name _____   Date _____

Good "NUT"rition

Johnny survived in winter by eating butternuts. Butternuts are a kind of walnut. Research some facts about nuts.

1. What is a nut?

   _____

   _____

2. Name some ways that nuts are healthy for you.

   _____

   _____

   _____

   _____

   _____

   _____

   _____

3. About how many calories are in one ounce (25 g) of nuts?

   _____

4. About how much fat is in one ounce (25 g) of nuts?

   _____

5. Are nuts higher or lower than fruit on the Food Guide Pyramid? What does that mean?

   _____

Food Guide Pyramid

A Guide to Daily Food Choices

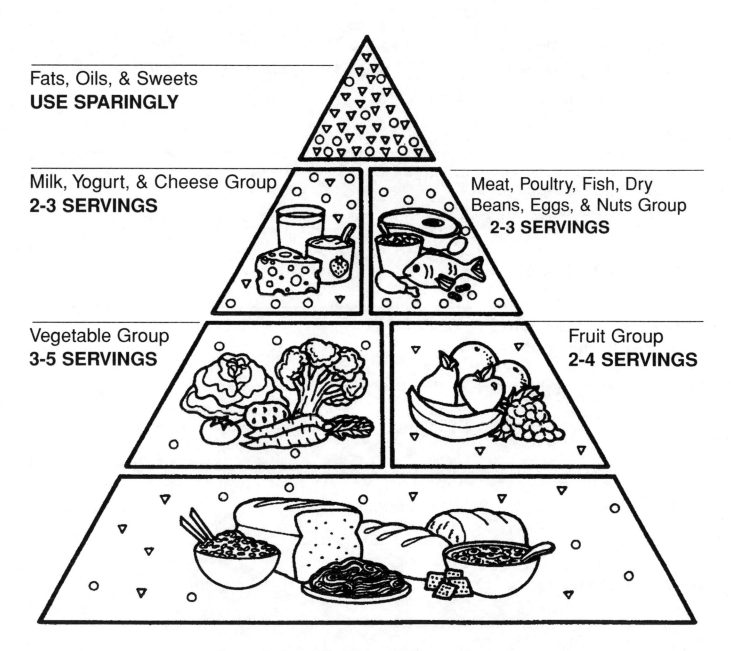

Fats, Oils, & Sweets
USE SPARINGLY

Milk, Yogurt, & Cheese Group
2-3 SERVINGS

Meat, Poultry, Fish, Dry
Beans, Eggs, & Nuts Group
2-3 SERVINGS

Vegetable Group
3-5 SERVINGS

Fruit Group
2-4 SERVINGS

Bread, Cereal, Rice, & Pasta Group
6-11 SERVINGS

Each of these food groups provides some, but not all, of the nutrients you need. No one food group is more important than another. For good health, you need them all. Go easy on fats, oils, and sweets, the foods in the small tip of the pyramid. You will get all the calories and sugar you need from the other foods on the pyramid.

Recipe for Applesauce

This recipe makes four servings.

Ingredients:

- 4 medium apples
- ½ cup (125 mL) water
- ⅓ cup (85 mL) granulated sugar
- ¼ tsp. (1 mL) ground cinnamon
- ⅛ tsp. (.5 mL) ground nutmeg

Preparation:

Wash and peel apples.
Remove core and stem.
Cut apples into fourths.
Heat apples and water to boiling over medium heat.
After apples and water boil, lower heat.
Simmer, uncovered, stirring to break up apples (5-10 minutes).
Add sugar, cinnamon, and nutmeg.
Heat all ingredients to boiling and stir for one minute.

Vocabulary: ingredients, boil, simmer, stir

Apple Dolls

Following are the directions for making an apple doll.

Materials:

- one firm apple
- potato peeler or paring knife (only used by an adult)
- scissors
- fabric
- seeds or beads
- paint and paintbrush
- glue
- yarn, string, cotton balls, or steel wool
- plastic dish detergent bottle (empty, clean, and dry)

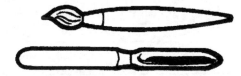

Directions for Making the Head:

1. Peel the apple, but leave the core in it.
2. Cut small slits for the eyes and mouth.
3. Let the apple dry for about four or five days.
4. Pinch the center of the apple to make a nose and let it dry for another week. When the apple feels hard and is a yellowish-brown color, it is dry enough.

Directions for Making the Doll:

1. Press in the eyes using seeds and beads.
2. Paint the lips, cheeks, and eyebrows.
3. Glue on hair using yarn, string, cotton balls, or steel wool.
4. Make the body from the dish detergent bottle.
5. Glue on fabric to cover the body.
6. Glue the head to the body.

Name _____   Date _____

Johnny's Forest Friends

Look carefully at the picture. See how many of Johnny's friends you can find. Fill in the graph. Then, answer the questions at the bottom of the page.

1. How many raccoons are there? _____

2. How many owls are there? _____

3. How many squirrels are there? _____

4. How many birds are there? _____

5. How many deer are there? _____

Name _____ Date _____

Where Is That?

Use the two maps on the next page to follow the directions below.

On the Top Map

1. Johnny was born in Leominster, Massachusetts.

    Draw a red apple on Leominster.

2. Johnny traveled to Ohio to plant apple orchards.

    Color Ohio green.

3. Johnny walked hundreds of miles through the Pennsylvania forests.

   Color Pennsylvania orange.

4. The settlers feared that Indians would attack them from Lake Erie.

    Color Lake Erie blue.

5. Johnny died near Fort Wayne, Indiana.

    Draw a yellow apple in Indiana.

6. When Johnny left home, in which direction did he travel to plant apple orchards?

On the Bottom Map:

After Johnny died, many people said they saw him in the states listed below. Find each state and draw an apple in it.

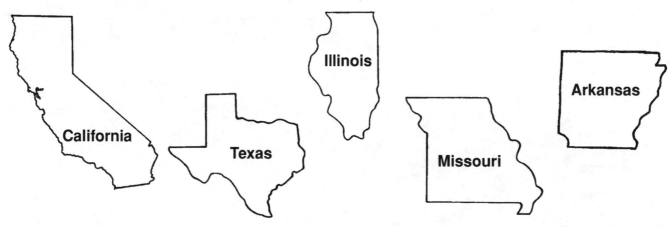

Name _____   Date _____

Where Is That? *(cont.)*

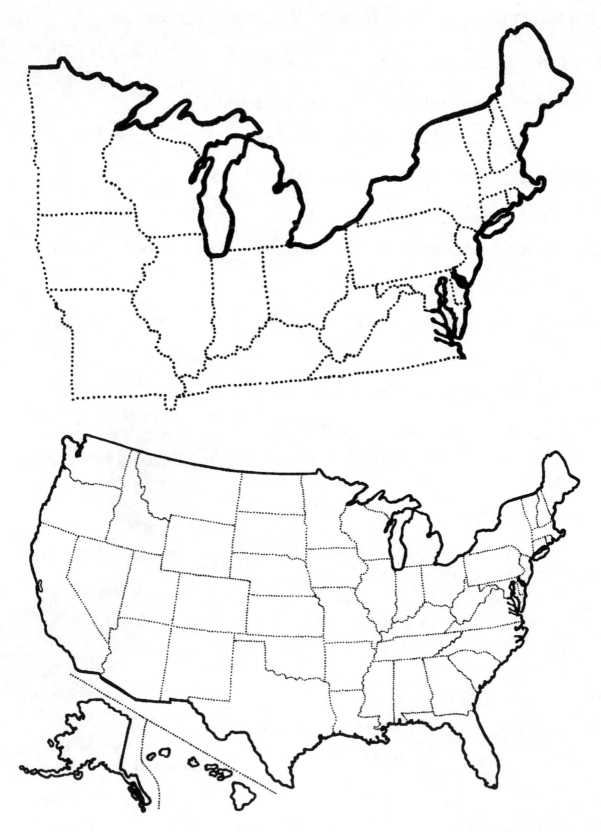

Name _____ Date _____

Movin' On!

Design a travel poster that would make people want to leave Massachusetts and move to Ohio in 1795.

What Would Johnny Do?

Teacher Note: See the directions on page 9, number 32.

1. A group of students line up for lunch. One student cuts in front of the others.

2. Two children are playing a game. A third child wants to play but also wants to change the rules.

3. One child is having a birthday party and is passing out invitations to some, but not all, of the class.

4. Two children want the same book at the library and both reach for it at the same time.

5. Several children are working in a group on a messy project, and one child refuses to help clean up.

6. One child pushes another for no reason and makes the second child fall.

What Would Johnny Do? *(cont.)*

7. There is a new student in class, and she does not speak English. She is always alone.

8. One child takes another child's pencil box. The second child is upset about it. A third child saw who took the pencil box.

9. There is a boy in class who always wants to fight. He is beating up a boy who is smaller than him. You see it.

10. Someone in class does not read well aloud. Two children start laughing at the child while reading.

11. A new girl goes to your school, and she has a physical challenge. Everyone avoids her because they think she cannot do anything.

12. Another child made up a lie about you. Now, no one will play with you. You know it is not true, but you feel very upset.

Nutty Gameboard

Teacher Note: See the directions on page 9, number 33.

Johnny Appleseed Readers' Theater

Announcer: Welcome to our readers' theater adaptation of *Johnny Appleseed*, a folktale retold by Steven Kellogg.

Cast of Characters:

Announcer	Mother	Man 2
Narrator 1	Three Indians	Old Hunter
Narrator 2	Woodsmen	Johnny's Family
Narrator 3	Woman	Children
Johnny	Man 1	Father

Narrator 1: On September 26, 1774, a little boy named John Chapman was born in Leominster, Massachusetts. As he grew up, he became known as *Johnny Appleseed*.

Narrator 2: Johnny's life was hard. His father left to fight in the Revolutionary War when Johnny was very young. His mother and baby brother died before Johnny was two years old.

Narrator 3: By the time Johnny turned six, his father had remarried. The new family settled in Longmeadow, Massachusetts. Within 10 years, there were 10 new brothers and sisters for Johnny.

Mother: Johnny, will you go pick some apples from the orchard? I think that I would like to make some applesauce with dinner tonight.

Johnny: My favorite! Sure!

Narrator 1: Johnny went out to the orchard and returned a few minutes later. He handed the apples to his mother.

Mother: Tomorrow, I would like you to start picking all the apples. After all, winter will be here soon, and I want to store as many as we can in the cellar. We want to have plenty of apple butter and apple pie when it is cold and snowy.

Johnny: Sure, Mom. I will do it first thing in the morning. I should have them all picked in a couple of days. I think I will go out and play now.

Narrator 2: Johnny loved to play in the woods. It was so quiet compared to his noisy house. He loved animals and just about everything in nature. The animals liked him, too.

Narrator 3: One day, when Johnny was a little older, he announced to his family that he was going away.

Johnny: I want to travel west and plant apple trees. New settlers are moving to Ohio, and I want them to have beautiful apple orchards like we have here. I will bring seeds from the cider mills. I'll be fine. You know I am very good at finding my way through woods.

Johnny Appleseed
Readers' Theater *(cont.)*

Narrator 1: Johnny's parents did not want him to go, but they knew that Johnny loved being outdoors and that he knew how to take care of himself. They also knew that he loved apples and that every seed he planted turned into a wonderful apple tree.

Father: Well, be careful and do not forget to write to us.

Family: Bye, Johnny. Good luck.

Narrator 2: Johnny walked hundreds of miles through the Pennsylvania forest. He cleared land and planted apple orchards. One day, while he was chopping a tree, he noticed three Indians watching him curiously.

Three Indians: *(All three look at Johnny and at each other with puzzled expressions on their faces.)*

Johnny: Hello, there.

Three Indians: *(They give no response.)*

Johnny: I am planting apple trees. Here, try an apple. Please.

Three Indians: (Cautiously, they hold out their hands. Each takes a bite. They smile, eat the apple faster, and begin to laugh. One of the Indians takes off his necklace and gives it to Johnny. They all shake hands.)

Narrator 3: After that, Johnny was good friends with the Indians.

Narrator 1: Another time, he came upon a gang of woodsmen. They tried to get Johnny to wrestle with them, but Johnny outsmarted them.

Woodsmen: Hey you, do you like to wrestle? We are the best. I'll bet you can't beat us!

Johnny: I have a better idea. Let's have a tree-chopping match. Let's see who can chop the most trees.

Woodsmen: That sounds like fun! (All woodsmen begin chopping.)

Johnny: Well, that was an easy way to clear the land. Look at them. They are all exhausted. Great!

Narrator 2: During the next few years, John continued to move westward. Whenever he ran out of apple seeds, he hiked back to the eastern cider presses to get more seeds. Before long, John's plantings were spread across the state of Ohio.

Narrator 3: Soon, pioneer families started to arrive.

Woman Say, what are those little trees?

Johnny: Apple trees. Here, take one. Here is one for you, too. Soon, you will have apple orchards and apples to eat every day. Have an apple.

Child: Thank you. Mmm, delicious!

Johnny Appleseed
Readers' Theater *(cont.)*

Child Two: Thanks. What is your name? Do you know any stories?

Johnny: Of course. I am John Chapman. I will tell you some stories tonight. Right now I am going to see if your ma and pa need any help.

Child Three: Your name should be *Johnny Appleseed*.

Narrator 1:   John went out of his way to help his new neighbors. He helped build their cabins. At night, he gathered all the children together and told them about his adventures. Sometimes he read stories from the Bible. Soon, they all were calling him Johnny Appleseed.

Narrator 2:   1812, the British incited the Indians to join them in another war against the Americans. Johnny did not like to see his friends fighting. One time, he even warned the settlers when he thought they were in danger.

Narrator 3:   After the war, everyone wanted Johnny to build a house for himself so he could live among them, but Johnny wanted to go back to live in the forest that he loved. However, sometimes he came back for a visit.

Narrator 1:   When he was gone, people would tell their favorite stories about Johnny. Sometimes, they would exaggerate a bit. For example, …

Woman: I remember when he was sleeping in a treetop hammock and chatting with the birds.

Man 1:   I remember when a rattlesnake attacked his foot, but his feet were so tough from walking that the snake's fangs could not go through.

Man 2:   That's nothing. I remember when he tended a wounded wolf and then kept the wolf for a pet.

Old Hunter: You should have seen him playing with a bear family.

Narrator 2:   As the years passed, Ohio became very crowded, so Johnny moved to Indiana. He continued to plant apple orchards there.

Narrator 3:   March of 1845, when Johnny was just over 70, he became sick for the first time in his life. He took shelter in a settler's cabin. Within a few days, he died.

Narrator 1:   Curiously, Johnny's stories continued to move westward without him. People said they saw him in Illinois and Missouri. Others were certain that he had planted trees in California. In fact, just today we thought we saw someone who looked like Johnny Appleseed. He dropped a sack right outside our door and ran away. Let's see what is inside. Wow! Maybe it was Johnny. Look at all these apples! *(The narrators pass out the apples to the audience.)*

Announcer: Thank you all for coming to see our show. Enjoy your apples. Remember to save the seeds and maybe you can plant a tree, too.

Music and Poetry

Old Brass Wagon

1. Circle to the left, the Old Brass Wagon,
    Circle to the left, the Old Brass Wagon,
    Circle to the left, the Old Brass Wagon,
    You're the one, my darling.

2. Swing, oh swing around, the Old Brass Wagon,
    Swing, oh swing around, the Old Brass Wagon,
    Swing, oh swing around, the Old Brass Wagon,
    You're the one, my darling.

Chorus: Promenade to right, the Old Brass Wagon,
    Promenade to right, the Old Brass Wagon,
    Promenade to right, the Old Brass Wagon,
    You're the one, my darling.

3. Walk it up and down, the Old Brass Wagon,
    Walk it up and down, the Old Brass Wagon,
    Walk it up and down, the Old Brass Wagon,
    You're the one, my darling.

4. Break and swing around, the Old Brass Wagon,
    Break and swing around, the Old Brass Wagon,
    Break and swing around, the Old Brass Wagon,
    You're the one, my darling.

Chorus: Promenade to right, the Old Brass Wagon,
    Promenade to right, the Old Brass Wagon,
    Promenade to right, the Old Brass Wagon,
    You're the one, my darling.

The music for this song can be found in *America Sings,* a musical collection edited by Carl Carmer and published by Alfred A. Knopf in 1942.

Two Little Apples

Way, way up in an apple tree
Two little apples smiled at me.
I shook that tree as hard as I could,
Down came those apples—
Ummmm, they were good!

– *Anonymous*

Teacher Note: To perform movements with the poem, do the following. At line one, stretch both arms high overhead. At line two, clench both fists to represent apples. At line three, shake your body all around. At line four, stoop to the floor, touching the floor with your fists. Finally, at line five, rub your stomach to show how delicious those apples were.

Bibliography

Fiction

Aliki. ***The Story of Johnny Appleseed.*** (Aladdin Paperbacks, 1987)

Burnett, Frances Hodgson. ***The Secret Garden.*** (Troll, 1988)

Krauss, Ruth. ***The Carrot Seed.*** (Harper Trophy, 1989)

Prelutsky, Jack. ***The Random House Book of Poetry for Children.*** (Random House, 2000)

Romanova, Natalia. ***Once There Was a Tree.*** (EP Dutton, 1992)

Silverstein, Shel. ***The Giving Tree.*** (HarperCollins, 1966)

Udry, Janice May. ***A Tree Is Nice.*** (Harper Trophy, 1987)

Barker, Cicely Mary. ***Flower Fairies of the Garden.*** (Warne Frederick & Co., 1997)

Roberts, Bethany. ***The Wind's Garden.*** (Henry Halt & Co., Inc, 2001)

Tep, Lawrence. ***Tree of Dreams.*** (Bridge Water Books. 1996)

Nonfiction

Maestro, Betsy. ***How Do Apples Grow?*** (Harper Trophy, 1993)

Micucci, Charles. ***The Life and Times of the Apple.*** (Orchard Books, 1995)

Nottridge, Rhoda. ***Apples.*** (Carolrhoda Books, 1991)

Schneiper, Claudia. ***An Apple Tree Through the Year.*** (Carolrhoda, 1988)

Cole, Henry. ***Jack's Garden.*** (Mulberry Books, 1997)

Talmage, Ellan. ***Unearthing Garden Mysteries: Experiments for Kids.*** (Fulcrum, 2000)

Carle, Eric. ***The Tiny Seed.*** (Aladdin, 2001)

Other Books by Steven Kellogg *(partial list)*

Chicken Little. (Morrow, 1987)

The Christmas Witch. (Puffin, 2000)

Mike Fink. (Mulberry Books, 1998)

The Mysterious Tadpole. (Dial, 1993)

Paul Bunyan. (Morrow, 1985)

Pecos Bill. (Mulberry Books, 1992)

A Rose for Pinkerton. (EP Dutton, 1993)

Answer Key

Page 16: My Special Place

1. He went to the woods.
2. The forest was peaceful.

Pages 18-19: True or Tall?

True

You can pick apples from trees.

You can survive on butternuts and apples.

You can sometimes outsmart troublemakers.

You can make friends with strangers.

You can make applesauce, cider, and vinegar from apples.

You can store apples in a cool cellar to eat all winter.

Tall

You can walk hundreds of miles barefoot in the snow without harm.

You can talk to birds, and they will understand.

You can keep a wild wolf for a pet.

People still see Johnny Appleseed today.

The skin on your feet can be so tough a rattlesnake cannot bite through it.

You can play with bears that you meet in a forest.

Page 22: Safey First

1. In a snowstorm, Johnny found shelter or built a lean-to.
2. He ate butternuts.
3. Johnny did not get lost because he could follow the trail of his orchards. He also knew the woods and wilderness well.

Pages 23-24: Pack Your Back

55 lbs. or 25 kg.

Page 28: Just for Fun

```
C L E A R E D B F U X F V T
B X Y N B M R Y U N R R H U
E R E C O L L E C T I O N S
L A J I I E E M R A J N Y H
O C B D S J A G B M N T Y E
V T K E T U N M T E B I E L
E I B R E Y T C D D M E X T
D C F P R N O X Z R I R L E
B A N R O V R O U T E S Z R
R L J E U T R U D G I N G K
V F M S S K G R I E V E D S
J K E S W I L D E R N E S S
```

Page 29: Vocabulary Quiz

1. inspired
2. penetrate
3. butternuts
4. boasted
5. exaggerated
6. replenish
7. grieved
8. urged
9. tranquil
10. wilderness

Page 31: An Apple a Day

1. Answers will vary.
2. 80 calories
3. almost none
4. It is fibrous, juicy, and not sticky. The mechanical act of eating an apple also helps clean the teeth.
5. 2-4 servings

Page 32: Good "NUT"rition

1. A nut is a dry fruit that has a hard shell and a kernel inside.
2. Answers will vary.
3. 170 calories
4. 528 oz. or 19g
5. They are higher. You will need more fruits than nuts.

Page 36: Johnny's Forest Friends

4 raccoons; 2 owls; 3 squirrels; 4 birds; 1 deer